Pebble®
Plus

FAVORITE
DESIGNER
DOGS

You'll
Love Chiweenies

by Erin Edison

Gail Saunders-Smith PhD,
Consulting Editor

CAPSTONE PRESS
a capstone imprint

Pebble Plus is published by Capstone Press,
1710 Roe Crest Drive, North Mankato, Minnesota 56003
www.capstonepub.com

Library of Congress Cataloging-in-Publication Data
Edison, Erin, author.
  You'll love chiweenies / Erin Edison.
     pages cm.—(Favorite designer dogs) (Pebble plus)
  Summary: "Simple text and full-color photographs describe the characteristics and care of the Chiweenie, a cross between a Chihuahua and Dachshund."—Provided by publisher.
  Includes bibliographical references and index.
  ISBN 978-1-4914-0567-3 (hb)—ISBN 978-1-4914-0635-9 (pb)—ISBN 978-1-4914-0601-4 (eb)
1. Chiweenie—Juvenile literature. 2. Toy dogs—Juvenile literature. 3. Dog breeds—Juvenile literature. I. Title. II. Title: You will love chiweenies.
  SF429.C49E35 2015
  636.76—dc23   2014001360

Editorial Credits
Erika L. Shores, editor; Kyle Grenz, designer; Katy LaVigne, production specialist

Photo Credits
Capstone Studio: Karon Dubke, cover, 11, 17; Glow Images: Superstock/Damon Craig, 1, 19, 21; iStockphotos: DeborahMaxemow, 13; MCT via Getty Images: Fort Worth Star-Telegram/Jill Johnson, 15; Shutterstock: Gelpi JM, 5 (bottom), Lee319, 7, Sergey Lavrentev, 5 (top); Wikipedia: Cgoodell, 9

Design Elements
Shutterstock: Julynx

Note to Parents and Teachers

The Favorite Designer Dogs series supports national science standards related to life science. This book describes and illustrates Chiweenies, a cross between a Chihuahua and a Dachshund. The images support early readers in understanding the text. The repetition of words and phrases helps early readers learn new words. This book also introduces early readers to subject-specific vocabulary words, which are defined in the Glossary section. Early readers may need assistance to read some words and to use the Table of Contents, Glossary, Read More, Internet Sites, and Index sections of the book.

Printed in the United States of American in North Mankato, Minnesota.
042014   008087CGF14

Table of Contents

What Is a Chiweenie? 4

The Chiweenie Look 8

Puppy Time 14

Caring for Chiweenies 16

Tiny Watchdogs 20

Glossary 22

Read More 23

Internet Sites 23

Index 24

What Is a Chiweenie?

A Chiweenie is a designer dog.
Designer dogs are a mix of
two purebreds. A Chihuahua
and a Dachshund make
a Chiweenie.

Chihuahua

Dachshund

5

People sometimes call
Dachshunds "wiener dogs."
This nickname makes up
the second part of the
Chiweenie's name.

The Chiweenie Look

Chiweenies are small dogs.
Adult Chiweenies weigh up
to 10 pounds (4.5 kilograms).
They stand just 8 inches
(20 centimeters) tall.

Chiweenies look like a mix
of their parent breeds. Most have
large Chihuahua ears and eyes.
But Chiweenies get their long,
low backs from the Dachshund.

Chiweenies can be brown, black, or tan. They can also be a mix of colors. Coats are short or medium in length.

Puppy Time

Chiweenies in a litter often don't look alike. Each puppy can be a different color. Puppies are adults after 18 months. Chiweenies can live 15 years.

Caring for Chiweenies

Chiweenies are playful and brave. But they're too small for rough play. Their long backs make them more likely to get hurt.

It is important to train Chiweenies to sit and stay. They need to learn not to jump from high places. Jumping can hurt their long backs.

Tiny Watchdogs

Chiweenies are loyal pets.

They often will yap if anything

comes near their families.

Chiweenies watch out

for their owners.

Glossary

brave—showing courage and willingness to do difficult things

breed—a certain kind of animal within an animal group

coat—an animal's hair or fur

litter—a group of animals born at the same time to the same mother

loyal—being true to something or someone

purebred—having parents of the same breed

training—teaching an animal to do what you say

Read More

Ganeri, Anita. *Dogs.* A Pet's Life. Chicago: Heinemann Library, 2009.

Shores, Erika L. *All About Chihuahuas.* Dogs, Dogs, Dogs. North Mankato, Minn.: Capstone Press, 2013.

Slade, Suzanne. *Why Do Dogs Drool?: And Other Questions Kids Have About Dogs.* Kids' Questions. Minneapolis: Picture Window Books, 2010.

Internet Sites

FactHound offers a safe, fun way to find Internet sites related to this book. All of the sites on FactHound have been researched by our staff.

Here's all you do:

Visit *www.facthound.com*

Type in this code: 9781491405673

Check out projects, games and lots more at
www.capstonekids.com

Index

backs, 10, 16, 18

bravery, 16

breeds, 10

Chihuahuas, 4, 10

coats, 12

colors, 12, 14

Dachshunds, 4, 6, 10

ears, 10

eyes, 10

jumping, 18

life spans, 14

litters, 14

loyalty, 20

owners, 20

playfulness, 16

puppies, 14

purebreds, 4

size, 8, 16

training, 18

weight, 8

wiener dogs, 6

Word Count: 202
Grade: 1
Early-Intervention Level: 14